A Heavenly Echo

A Heavenly Echo

The Twelve Steps in Christian Reflection

DAN BALLINGER

Foreword by S. Gus Lee

RESOURCE *Publications* • Eugene, Oregon

A HEAVENLY ECHO
The Twelve Steps in Christian Reflection

Copyright © 2016 Dan Ballinger. All rights reserved. Except for brief quotations in critical publications or reviews, no part of this book may be reproduced in any manner without prior written permission from the publisher. Write: Permissions, Wipf and Stock Publishers, 199 W. 8th Ave., Suite 3, Eugene, OR 97401.

Resource Publications
An Imprint of Wipf and Stock Publishers
199 W. 8th Ave., Suite 3
Eugene, OR 97401

www.wipfandstock.com

PAPERBACK ISBN 13: 978-1-4982-8450-9
HARDCOVER ISBN 13: 978-1-4982-8452-3

Manufactured in the U.S.A.   04/29/2016

Unless otherwise noted, Scripture is the author's paraphrase.

Scripture marked "MSG" taken from *The Message*. Copyright © 1993, 1994, 1995, 1996, 2000, 2001, 2002. Used by permission of NavPress Publishing Group.

Scripture marked "NASB" taken from the NEW AMERICAN STANDARD BIBLE®, Copyright © 1960, 1962, 1963, 1968, 1971, 1972, 1973, 1975, 1977, 1995 by The Lockman Foundation. Used by permission.

Scripture marked "KJV" taken from the King James Version. Public Domain.

Contents

Foreword by S. Gus Lee | vii
Preface | ix
Introduction | xv

STEP ONE
Facing Life's Unmanageability | 1

STEP TWO
Coming to Believe | 7

STEP THREE
Saying Yes to God | 13

STEP FOUR
Living in the Light:
Beginning Self-Acceptance and Self-Awareness | 17

STEP FIVE
No Longer Alone | 20

STEP SIX
Deep Desire for God's Influence | 24

STEP SEVEN
Walking the Talk, by Faith | 28

STEP EIGHT
Developing a Conscience | 32

STEP NINE
Developing Skill in Relationships | 34

STEP TEN
Ongoing Self-Acceptance and Perfectionism | 36

STEP ELEVEN
Growing God-Consciousness, Seeking the Impossible | 39

STEP TWELVE
Amazing Grace: Knowing and Sharing Our God-Life | 43

POSTSCRIPT
Humanity beyond Sobriety, Time-Space, and Death | 49

Bibliography | 63

Foreword

Dan was well into his retirement years when I first met him, having served in pastoral ministry for twenty years, then in Christian counseling for thirty more. Dan and Norma, his wife of nearly fifty years, came to my organization volunteering their vast experience and maturity.

I was in a dark place. My wife had had a complete emotional breakdown. Our fourth child had just been born into our toxic atmosphere of confusion, anxiety, anger, and frustration. I'd felt my fifteen years of ministry and my very sense of calling sabotaged. My core identities that had given me pride and meaning in life—husband, father, and missionary—had all failed me. Countless nights I went to sleep wishing to never wake up.

Almost a decade since, Dan has helped me to accept the absurdity and error in self-reliance and self-control in responding to the powerful forces, lies, strongholds, and situations in my life. He has coached me to enter into a place of full dependency on the God I knew then, and the God I have come to experience in greater intimacy now. But perhaps more importantly, he has modeled life for me.

That he overcame the destructive trajectory of his childhood affected by alcoholism, abuse, and divorce gave me the impulse to dig in and stay the course. That he and Norma came out victorious through the first twenty years of very difficult marriage gave me

Foreword

hope for my own. And after a life full of struggles with addiction and challenges in his own family, that this seasoned octogenarian still chose to remain open, honest, and ready to own his shortcomings and mistakes taught me a thing or two about humility. He allowed me, thirty years his junior, to enter into his life as an equal, and what had started as a counseling relationship became a friendship.

This *life* is evident in his writing. It would be easy to overlook a book on the Twelve Steps for those of us who have not struggled with chemical dependency. But this book, to be sure, is not only about recovery from addiction but about recovering the power of the gospel in responding to all kinds of human conditions. Dan's weighty, succinct prose takes us on a journey of discovery of God's handiwork that far surpasses any individual recovery or salvation, into the greater realm of the gospel of his eternal kingdom.

Dan presents the Twelve Steps for what they are—the work of the Holy Spirit. The Spirit, through a few desperate men, birthed it. It is still the Spirit who drives us toward something (Someone) greater than ourselves in overcoming life's challenges.

This book is about the gospel of the kingdom of God: that in his infinite wisdom, God chose to use the frail, the addicted, the dysfunctional, the diseased, the marginalized, the suicidal, and the rest of us who were stuck in our own humanity to redeem his creation. Through this book, Dan starts us off on a journey of the impossible, of rescuing the hopeless and turning our eyes to the only thing that truly matters—our relationship with the King of all creation.

S. Gus Lee
Frontier Ventures*

---

* Formerly U.S. Center for World Mission

Preface

Much of my reason for discussing the Twelve Steps and the Christian faith together is that they have the potential to throw a great deal of light on each other. I first began to realize this in 1987 when I joined the national Christian twelve-step organization, Overcomers Outreach, founded by Bob and Pauline Bartosch two years earlier. I was the son of an alcoholic father; I was also an ordained minister and a pastoral counselor receiving further psychological training at the time. Over the next ten years I was to be introduced to some remarkable people and principles through the twelve-step program and to its power to improve my life, family, and vocation. My hope is to discuss these principles in ways that will encourage some Christians to use the Steps to improve their discipleship to Christ. Conversely, I wish to encourage non-Christian Twelve Steppers to consider the value of the great gospel truths that were screened out of the Alcoholics Anonymous (AA) program but aren't necessarily in conflict with it.

My first encounter with the Twelve Steps was in a Christian twelve-step organization, but others followed that were not church related. I spent several years in an ACA or ACoA (Adult Child of Alcoholics) group along with training under Bill Ritchie, a licensed chemical-dependency counselor. These associations expanded my self-awareness and applications of my biblical faith.

Preface

These thirty years of fruitful, happy experience since have encouraged me as a Christian family member and minister toward more honesty and humility. They have also inspired in me a deeper appreciation of the Christian faith and its vital relationship with many life-recovery movements—some of which are wrongly thought of as outside that faith.

But if such a movement is seen as parachurch or somehow separate, it is because its existence is virtually necessitated by the Christian church's weakness in many areas where the church was originally created to serve humanity. I will speak only briefly of how the earliest church, undivided and spiritually powerful, was corrupted. That first-century apostolic church lived and heralded a vital faith in a man (Christ) risen from the dead, one who offered his living presence in local gatherings of ordinary people. These ordinary people were empowered in their meetings by the experience of extraordinary gifts of his Spirit for healing, hope, and love.

This rapidly spreading people movement became a large part of the Roman Empire within less than a hundred years (10 percent or more by AD 120). With its popularity came a diluting of its original self-submitting faith character. As its influence and numbers increased, so did the self-serving motivations for joining it. Following Christ came to mean more—less, actually—than giving one's life to Christ in loving service. As this trend continued in an increasingly powerful and wealthy community, the community's imitation of the empire it was overtaking politically also gathered momentum. The church developed many traits that served the preservation of an empire much more than they did a humble faith community.

The first parachurch movements in those earliest centuries began in reaction to this corrupting and politicizing of Christianity. Monastic movements (parachurch) and a church hierarchy developed side by side. The monasteries were trying to maintain the life Christ actually taught, and the hierarchy was trying to keep the church's increasingly Christless life from completely dying out. The hierarchy's power just grew and grew. By the fourth century and the arrival of the quasi-Christian Emperor Constantine,

Preface

Christianity was the official religion of the Roman Empire, and it would be a thousand years before this sad marriage between church and state even began to dissolve. Its dissolution is still in progress today wherever there are Christians. The parachurch and extra church movements have been and always will be surging out from this adulterated, squabbling main church body.

Following in the historical footsteps of this long line of renewal energy has come the vital and life-restoring twelve-step movement. This and Christ's gospel are of one family in God, I believe. Their common starting point is, as Richard Rohr has so saliently pointed out, the issue of sin (in the Bible's terminology), which lies right alongside the issue of addiction (in the AA's). These different terms create an apparent church/AA divergence, but Rohr's poignant resolution is to note that sin, like addiction, is a disease.[2] We humans are all addicted to things less life-building than God's Spirit and plan. But as Jesus said, he came not for those who were well but for the sick.

My experience with the Twelve Steps as a Christian these past thirty years has been very positive. It has led me to see that the original charter of the gospel, which was to heal such addictions, has been greatly weakened in practice. The gospel was intended to do for us the very life recovery that AA does rather broadly. The genius of Bill Wilson and his early AA cofounders was that they cut their community loose from the theoretical, doctrinal squabbling of the weakened church. They were faith men, influenced by the Oxford Movement in the Anglican Church, who were desperate for sobriety on earth, not for a theoretical path to a future bliss in heaven. They did not start a parachurch organization for addiction (like Teen Challenge, for instance). They established a specific spiritual program for people at the "bottom" in life who could hear hope in a "higher power," a God as they understood God. They gave up doctrines of afterlife bliss for practical help with this-life normalcy. They said that religion was for people avoiding hell; spirituality was for people who had been there.

---

2. Rohr, *Breathing Under Water*.

Preface

The amazing dynamic here, which will form the theme of this book, is that the founders infused into the Steps the heart and spirit of their people's ancient faith while cutting out so much of its historical baggage. And it worked. The heart and spirit was enough for millions of people around the world. I would like to say just a little more about what I think this "heart and spirit" of the gospel is and then probe the Steps as they relate to that Christian spirit.

Stated clearly, the gospel as historical reality is unique among all religions; the welfare of all humanity hinges on the meaning and benefits of the resurrection of Jesus of Nazareth two thousand years ago. The meaning and benefits of this powerful event are the basis of the heart and spirit of Christian belief. How that heart and spirit is related to the Twelve Steps and all such beneficial programs is beautifully expressed in the Old Testament account of King David's encounter with the woman of Tekoa (2 Sam 14:1–20). She appeals to her king, David, to return his son Absalom from exile. She uses a made-up story about her two sons fighting; one kills the other, and now out of vengeance the family wants the remaining son to die. In her storytelling she speaks some beautiful, poignantly moral prose, among it the phrase, "Yet God does not take away life, but devises means by which his banished be not far from him" (v. 14).

This elegant turn of words expresses both the heart of the Christian phenomena and the basic spiritual energy of the twelve-step movement. It also tells much of how the AA program (and other spiritual renewals) sprang out of the Christian movement; it is not a stretch to see this "devising of [varied, creative] means" for reaching out to the suffering, including the addicted, as a historically consistent characteristic of God in Christianity. This is varyingly true of all religion, and indeed virtually every aspect of existence and natural human functions. Jesus taught that God—"the kingdom of heaven")—is like a dragnet cast into the sea, gathering fish, people, of every kind (Matt 13:47). God is out in our world "gathering," and the steps are part of that. Solomon echoes this in Ecclesiastes when he observes that God has worked in all

Preface

things so that men should revere him, rejoicing in their gifts, work, and goodness, with eternity in their hearts (Eccl 3:13–14).

So here is our theme for this book: seeing God in everything in our existence, but especially in our pain, as he calls and reaches out to us to get our attention, recover our humanity, and get us "home," so that we may be fully conscious of his caring presence in our lives.

Introduction

The theme of this book is that God is the primary agent in the grace that grants his life to the undeserving and previously uninterested. Grace such as this always needs explaining, because anyone can see that the Steps need to be *worked* in order to be effective; so it is natural to think that our working the Steps is what frees us from that which previously enslaved us. This view of God actively working in the Steps versus the Steps as mere tools is subtle but crucial. It is about the inner, spiritual relationship God wants to form with us through the Steps—in other words, the gospel's impact on our minds.

If we begin "walking the walk" or "believing" or "following" or whatever we might call it, thinking that our relationship to God is regulated by our complete understanding or compliance, we will eventually run dry; we will end up where we began, thinking we started a new program for life betterment. This is morality pure and simple, and it feeds the orientation toward self that brought us to powerlessness in the first place. It is religion without God, and fatal.

If, on the other hand, we begin by thinking that we experienced a miracle—that of hearing God's song, in which he invited us to a life of hearing him sing and author life's songs—then we will again arrive where we started, gleeful responders to God's performance. This kind of music is eternal in nature and endless in variety and renewal. It is about God and from God and for God, and knowing this even a little allows his Spirit song to be our ongoing soul music, enabling us to perennially continue as we began. This means doing the Steps, especially the first three, all our lives, being reconverted over and over, not as a formula but as the door he opens to us anew repeatedly. After powerlessness, God appears and calls to us in every challenge life presents as we knock on the door of these Steps, his power and his care flooding our deepest mind with the joy of serenity and safety. We are amazed at having friendship with God! In this way, and only in this way, can the Steps or gospel sustain us in feeding our innermost soul, which is never satisfied with a static way of relating to God. Ours must be a dynamic relationship, not a clever formula.

Why must it be dynamic? Because buried in and surging out of the Steps and the gospel is the reality that we are much more like God than we are different. What this means is that however sick our souls have become through addiction (or sin!), they are still capable of resonating with God's song from eternity. God sings this song in millions of melodies and harmonies and tonal frequencies, from within the tiniest particle or wave of energy, to the grandest sonnet of human creation or the most massive galaxy. We are made to be his audience, or to use another image, his Son's wife—an eternal, vibrant part of his true family, now and forever.

I realize my tone sounds somewhat pie-in-the-sky— but it does not sound that way to me in light of what God has done for my life these past thirty years. The Steps have become for me a meal I can share at any moment as I sit at table with this inexpressibly beauteous, kind, and resourceful ("resource-full") Soul-Shepherd.

"Perfect love casts out fear," Jesus's beloved apostle John wrote. No one can sing of this blessed release more than the child of alcoholics whose life was nearly destroyed by such fear —and rage—before love came beckoning through the Steps. I see him in them, persuading me against powerful, terrifying "truths," non-verbal realities, that moved my soul like a guided missile through the first thirty years of my life—and I not at all aware of them. I had learned to use anger rather than acknowledge my fear. I was

Introduction

ashamed of my fear. Slowly I have seen that fear, if I own it, can relate me more closely to those I love. Anger wounds, but fear can make me harmless and more human.

There are terrors in the deep mind that boggle that mind's power to name or comprehend them; they drive the soul with power beyond human limits. The First Step appeals to us who are wounded with an astonishing power to release us, and this relief makes us love its Author deeply. Our fear is reined in by "working" these Steps—that is, by turning them over internally in relation to the anxiety's cause. It is like Isaiah wrote—blessedly!—in a passage that he could have addressed to an alcoholic: "'Come now, and let us reason together,' says the LORD, 'Though your sins [thinking] are as scarlet ["stinking," misdirected], they will be as white as snow [clear and straight]'" (Isa 1:18 NASB).

This "working," this responsive relating, can result in a man—a husband, father, minister, etc.—who begins to change in ways that allow his family and friends to forgive him and graciously reconcile with him. When this makes his marriage a new, growing love affair over decades, this man resonates vibrantly with the song God gave to him.

So it can go for any Adult Child, and though I have friendships with alcoholics, I am not clear how such renewal is for them. I've gone on many "mission trips" in Long Beach and Los Angeles with recovering alcoholics who clearly do know how healing is for them pre- and post-recovery. I noticed that they talked very straight to the men there on Skid Row, and they explained to me that this is because deception and denial are endemic in the disease. It takes straight talk and a firm heart to get through such thick defenses.

Some family members may not be as thick skinned, and some of us will integrate our spirituality and the Steps a little more gracefully than the harder-hitting mode I saw there years ago and in various writings. It is likely that some of us feel more grace than work in working the Steps because of our theology or because we were quite broken by the time we first saw them. I only have my experience, which is limited, and I share it here as honestly

Introduction

as possible. I am a nondrinking member of an alcoholic family of origin and a Christian hoping to help others like me accept and use the Steps.

My desire is that this journey through the Steps will relate hope to some "up and outs" like myself, whose lives have been seriously endangered by sins that are hidden from public view but as painful as any recorded outwardly.

STEP ONE

Facing Life's Unmanageability

"We admitted that we were powerless over alcohol and that our lives had become unmanageable."

"Then the eyes of both of them were opened, and they knew that they were naked.... Then the LORD God called to the man, and said to him, 'Where are you?' He said, 'I heard the sound of You in the garden, and I was afraid because I was naked; so I hid myself.'"

—GENESIS 3:7,9–10 NASB

The Genesis story describing the functional source of our troubles in this world is widely associated with the religious baggage that Bill W. eliminated in formulating the Steps. Unfortunately, the narrative can be misused by Bible thumpers who think that scaring people is the way to introduce God into their lives.

A Heavenly Echo

I much prefer Rev. Richard Rohr's more enlightened approach in his book *Breathing Under Water*. He goes to the functional heart of our universal human struggle along with Bill W., but we are talking here and in Rohr's book and in the Steps about the same thing: the biblical concept of the "fall of man." Rohr's discussion of it is very wise and Step-like; he does not talk theology but life as any of us can observe it. It is true that life is confusing and largely upside down—but this language recasts and disguises the deeper truth that Rohr knows (which Bill W. also knew), that life is like this because humanity somehow lost its best, inner relationship long ago—its relationship with its Maker. Though Bill W. was never a church member, some of his friends were or had been at one time. Their Step thinking filtered out some church doctrine, but it retained several core Christian truths about relating consciously and honestly to God.

These great Steppers used words from outside the Bible to talk about this universal human tragedy. They did this to avoid the abuse of its mystery, already so widely committed by religious people in our Western spiritual history. The Steps are not a place for theological or philosophical debates. They are life preservers thrown into the deepest soul-waters at the moment before drowning.

The biblical message and the First Step say the same thing in different ways: there is something wrong with our world, and it is us! The problem for both messengers is that this "something wrong" carries shame about ourselves. The shame-damaged soul develops psychological defenses to survive in a shame-producing world, including in its family of origin. Some damages are so deep that no internal defense can keep the mind functioning; hence alcoholic use and abuse. All of these wounds produce self-defenses that make any talk of self-improvement painful. When the pain of our broken lives overpowers this "pride pain," then we are usually at our "bottom."

The world of society and religion is largely the human world of shame-directed behavior and self-identity. Guilt, (related to shame as neurosis is to psychosis in degree of seriousness, controls

Facing Life's Unmanageability

a great deal of the moral choice in our world. It walks the middle ground between two extremes: suicidal activity and sociopathic behavior on the negative side, and on the positive, beatifically creative, humanity-serving mission life.

The First Step, like all twelve, is an observation, not a preachment, from Bill's journey from shame to sobriety and beyond. It is not a manipulative preachment or moralizing or guilting. It is the report of a starving man who has found a source of food, free and endless, and is sharing this glad experience with other starving people. In actuality, the First Step agrees with the greatest religious minds and truths history has witnessed. The difference is that Bill W. skipped the part of their message that gravitated toward shame and guilt and struck directly at shame's life block. He said that we saw our *powerlessness*, or *sickness*—not badness, evilness, weakness, etc. We saw that we were controlled by something far more powerful than ourselves, something that had the power to render our lives unmanageable. We were brought to this addictive condition not because of shameful weakness of character but because for us, with our history and our chemistry, and so on, alcohol was a huge overpowering adversary. To miss this truth would only make us more ashamed (misguidedly so), and the more we felt ashamed, the more we needed alcohol to kill that pain.

This cycle of pain/shame, self-medication with alcohol, and shame again at the dependency, Bill W. implied, was what drove people to a life of unmanageability and insanity. Not being able to manage the drinking—like other people, "normal people," they secretly thought—stoked the hellish flames of shame ever more intensely. "Hellish" is not an exaggeration for those who've been trapped in this soul-killing cycle.

So in fact we are all talking about the death that the Genesis story reports. It was a death, God said, that would make the human soul thirsty for more than it understood or knew how to satisfy. To some degree this universal confusion pushes most of us to persist in pursuing an unreachable satisfaction. It is behind all of the topsy-turvy conflict we have in our selves and in society.

We are even pushed to the point of playing God in our desire to control life's outcomes.

For those of us poisoned by alcoholism, Bill W. presented a most precious gift when he startlingly passed over this complex psychospiritual conversation. He simply recognized the shame-defeating reality that alcohol was too powerful for some human beings to manage, and said that it was rational and wise to give up this form of playing God. By the time Bill W. wrote the First Step, he and his friends had experienced sobriety and a lot more, as the next eleven Steps describe. With this knowledge came the wisdom to design the Steps, with only this marvelous, soul-freeing admission as Step One. Bill W.'s depth of wisdom about human dynamics is the reason the Twelve Steps are so meaningful and helpful for people in general, not just addicts. This brings us back to our discussion of life's upside-down character. We are saying from the genesis that life's laws here are designed to narrow down on us as our own forms of addiction (sin) carry us toward potential total destruction.

God created us and our world to work in relation to him and his amazingly creative natural laws. When this order was overturned, the creation in us and our environment became "unmanageable." This state of affairs, Bill W. and Genesis agree, was designed to bring us to the admission of the reality of our powerlessness. And this admission would become the door opening once again to our real souls and to God. With addiction, we are bucking the laws guiding the universe's operation; our "bottom" is the end of our ability to maintain that struggle, and God waits there for us in the Steps like the father of the Prodigal Son.

We generally resist accepting the source of our troubles as powerlessness because of the defenses we have developed to protect our sense of worth. And any talk of our needing help with a "problem" seems aimed right at our self-worth. Bill W., however, aimed a word at our sense of worth that simultaneously protected it and described our problem: *powerlessness* is not by definition sinful or shameful, and when one has "bottomed," the meaning of the word is a relief to the addict expecting condemnation.

Facing Life's Unmanageability

Interventionists and chemical-dependency counselors know this. They typically use love language to couch frank (but not hostile) descriptions of dysfunctional behavior that shows a problem. Bill and his Big Book authors practiced this noncritical approach with alcoholics. Their language also filters out a lot of psychobabble, favoring the plain talk of their day.

The "plain talk" to which addicts are resistant until they hit bottom should include talk of sin as a form of addiction, as Rohr describes it. I'll use a little of it now in hopes of persuading non-substance abusing people that sin's universal effect renders each of us as desperate spiritually as any alcoholic. Sin, as Rohr says, is a disease like alcoholism, and deadly. The New Testament says that "the wages of sin is death" (Rom 6:23), and that a little of it soon becomes too much. The Steps echo the gospel in converting the soul, something every human soul urgently needs.

I illustrate the value of "plain talk" by telling of something I often wished with regard to my late addicted father. I had this wish only after I met God in a new way in the Steps, and years after my father's passing.

My dad experienced limited but significant healing in returning to the faith of his youth late in life; his healing came through a church community rather than a twelve-step program. This means to me that the same principles or laws of grace operate in many spiritual communities, though the Steps offer an avenue specifically for addicts.

In my progressive recovery I wished that my dad had one day come to me and said something like this: "Danny, I want to tell you something that has happened to me this last year. I know this will be hard for you to believe, but it's real, it happened. I met a group of people who are like me. None of us can drink like we want—it's hell to pay if we do, because we can't stop. They told me their stories about this sad fact, and I was amazed at how their stories were like mine. They showed me that not being able to drink in a civilized manner and not being able to stop didn't mean that I was a spineless S.O.B. with no willpower. It meant that we were powerless, not spineless—that we were up against a very powerful force in alcohol, and it was nothing to be ashamed of to get steamrollered by it. I met some very smart and sophisticated businesspeople who said that admitting this kind of powerlessness had changed their lives. And now with their help it has changed mine. Danny, all my life I've been ashamed, but I thought I was just mad or frustrated. Remember how I used to say, 'I can quit this anytime I want to'? Admitting I couldn't quit just made me feel more ashamed of myself; I could never say that, that I can't quit. That seemed terrible to me, and I'd rather be drunk—as I look back, I'd rather be *dead*—than a stupid, weak, sniveling bum, living proof that my folks were right about me all along. Drinking made my hell bearable sometimes, but now I see it was making it all worse. Danny, when I saw these people needing help, that's when I could admit that I did too, and it was nothing to be ashamed of. I was powerless, like them, not a weakling. Danny, when I saw the difference between powerlessness and weakness, it was like getting out of jail. Danny, I've learned many other great things this year through this Alcoholics Anonymous organization, but this is the great thing that started a whole new life for me. I'm not ashamed anymore of who or what I am, because I have these friends who aren't ashamed of me, and now I know why. This feeling is in me a lot now, and it helps me 'work the Steps,' as they say, and *I don't have to drink anymore*; I can feel this feeling a lot without drinking, and I don't have a hangover or a lot of other bad things!"

I've heard this testimony from others, blessedly, and I've said similar words about my inner thinking issues as an ACoA. Now we all say of ourselves, "Hi, I'm Dan and I'm an alcoholic," or "Hi, I'm Dan and I'm my problem." We feel strength and hope as "our people" understand what this new self-acceptance is: a humble badge of honor and of a better heart.

STEP TWO

Coming to Believe

"We came to believe in a Power greater than ourselves, able to restore us to sanity."

"Now faith is the assurance of things hoped for, the conviction of things not seen."

—Hebrews 11:L

It is appropriate for anyone commenting on Step Two to get into enlightenment as a general spiritual concept. And this step is about that, eventually; it is where this step about power and reality points when it speaks of sanity. But thank God (as you understand God) that these first Steppers kept their focus on something a "drunk" could recognize—the struggle for survival power, which produced so much insane thinking and acting in their lives in the first place. Bill W. was talking to captives of a very subtle ruler, one deep inside their own minds who controlled their thinking invisibly and anonymously. From the Christian perspective, Bill is innately aware of the "god of this world." In the language of Step Two, this god is being confronted by "a Power greater than" himself or us.

Years ago I attended a conference at Fuller Theological Seminary on spiritual dynamics in psychological healing. This was where I first heard of the published correspondence between Bill Wilson and Carl Jung, the famous psychiatrist. The excerpt I heard was from a letter Jung had written to Bill W., commenting on the spiritual nature of alcoholism. Jung was affirming AA dynamics. He went on to say that it would be unrealistic to expect any individual to cope with the sinister spiritual power in alcohol ("spirits"—literally) unless he or she was supported intimately by a special community. This would mean people who understood the dark power involved in their conflict.

Citing Jung here is not only intended to show that some very bright medical people agree with Step people about the "spiritual powers" involved in our struggles; I will continue this line of thought to argue that the struggle is not only with *a power* but with *power itself*.

Jesus said of this dark spiritual powerbroker (the god of this world), "The thief comes only to steal and kill and destroy; I came that they may have life" (John 10:10 NASB). This description of evil reveals one who deals maliciously in power as the first value in existence. It should not be surprising, then, if such a being's main object in our world was to control its citizens with this interpretation of reality—the perspective that life is really all about power. And this is in fact an interpretation of the biblical insight into humanity's dilemma, that in Eden our first parents became susceptible to this view of their Creator and of one another. After "biting" into this sinister survivalist view of life, "they knew that they were naked" . . . and they were afraid (Gen 3:7,10).

The story tells us that they came to see each other and God quite differently after believing that God was keeping the best part of existence from their knowledge. The serpent charges, "God knows that in the day you eat from it . . . you will be like God, knowing good and evil" (Gen 3:5 NASB). There is no real freedom with loyalty to God, the serpent intimates. He wants to control you by keeping you ignorant of what's really going on, of how he really operates. Take control, get power, and you will fulfill your own destiny. Life is dangerous—do something.

Bill W. and Genesis agree that "playing God" has been our natural human response to stress for longer than we can remember. The Bible also tells us that God knew how this would go, and that he issued the so-called "curse" to put lifesaving limits on our ultimately insane urge. This included our life's resulting difficulties and our mortality: "bad" things put in place to prevent worse things.

This account leaves out the Darwinian explanation for all struggle as the basic need for survival advantage (another book, another time), which, like a lot of Darwinian thinking, contains some truth but doesn't help any with addiction.

So, we are greatly dysfunctional, mortal beings who struggle against a universal condition. God uses this phenomenon in life to wear us down and end the breech, to reconcile our deep minds with him in restored trust. "God sent not his Son into the world to condemn the world; but that the world through Him might be saved" (John 3:17 KJV).

At this point I want to comment on how the Steps developed and the uncanny order they took. I always want to know more about those early Steppers' experiences in the year or more that they traversed the road of these Twelve Steps to sobriety and spiritual awakening. What an amazing, providentially driven eruption of spiritual energy! In writing the Steps, Bill and his friends were not proselytizing; they were reporting out of a diary of sorts. Isn't it enthralling to see the progression they moved through, from utter brokenness to a clean and sober existence? And that this all began in 1935 before spreading vigorously through Western societies, societies that were about to become the most substance abusing in their millennia-long history! Coincidence? Synchronicity? Or God, as we are coming to understand God? If that twentieth-century "intervention" doesn't shout GOD at you in capital letters, then how about the emergence of these crystal clear Steps out of

Bill's sobriety quest? Or how about the order and progressively bondage-breaking character of the Steps themselves, especially the first three?

Let me put it another way. Step One records a psychological breakthrough that is foundational for an addict. It is hard for all of us dysfunctionals to approach and accept the idea of help for our "problem": fear abounds, anxiety grips—but once we give in or catch a glimpse of the firm friendliness offered to us, it is like a window opening a hot and stuffy room to fresh, cool air. Relief begins to flood in, and for many of us "working" this Step in a challenging circumstance, the relief can be physiological, fast, and wonderful.

Such positive relief from stress sets our mentality toward the next Step very congruently. Relief from shame turns the mind from negative to positive and makes us more susceptible to belief in an object of hope. This specific hope is the opposite of our powerlessness, a power that has an actual short-term result—sanity. Here is the second level of giving up control, one of several such subtle shifts in the first three Steps. At this point many of us are willing to trade whatever we were stewing about before we began working Step One for the solid promise of sanity. We'll now settle for the reality of immediate sanity rather than trying to "play God" or insisting on a result we would have demanded previously. This first faint level of contentment, piled on the first-Step relief of shame, is setting us up nicely to decide for real submission to God.

But before commenting on that, let me elaborate on the "believe" dynamic of Step Two. Over time, those who crystallized the wording of the Steps out of their unique 1935 move toward sobriety surely realized that what they were doing was aligning their thinking and decision making with God—and with his laws, which ordered them and their world. Many of us have come to see this from working Steps Eleven and Twelve. (All Twelve Steps are interwoven, backward and forward.) Aligning ourselves with God means that believing God and growing in that belief is drawing us into the happy ways God had in mind and put into cosmic actuality when he set the creation in motion. The Steps are helping us to line up with the invisible God in visible, productive ways in the here and now: we find the priceless sanity that results from turning away from power as the goal of life to healing trust and fear-quenching love. *Alcoholics Anonymous* graphically shows that belief in self to control drinking was a death sentence for those addicts. They learned that any higher power, any understanding of God, was much better—just no more self.

"A Power greater than ourselves" now very quickly means a peaceful and hopeful approach in whatever is disturbing us and tempting us to "power up" in a win-lose mindset. At this point we are being marvelously tilted toward a surrender of power altogether; that power was the insistence that the outcomes we wanted must go our way. One step further and we'll be in the safest place in existence: in God's will and hands, in his consequence-determining power. This is his banquet. One more step and we'll be admitted as a family member, properly attired and grinning from ear to spiritual ear. Bring on the hors d'oeuvre of *decision*, the robe of "turning our will and our lives over," and the main course, which is "the care of God,"—Step Three.

But before walking into that dining room, I must briefly finish connecting the Second Step to the Third. Restored sanity may seem like a value all on its own, but it shimmers tantalizingly between powerlessness (Step One) and God's care (Step Three). Both of these are needed to form a solid sense of the "conscious contact with God" described in Step 11. In this way the first three Steps and the last two are more about aligning ourselves with God, while Steps Four through Ten are more about relating to ourselves and to other humans. Step Two, in this beginning trail of recognizing God's reality, is certainly about God-given spiritual perception, but I wish to consider "enlightenment" (Step Eleven) and sanity (Step Two) as slightly different things.

I said above that the sanity of Step Two connects very closely to Step Three, but that it is also seems like a value all on its own. This sanity value energetically anticipates the surrender in Step Three. These steps interconnect in a wonderfully fluid way, and Step Two sanity begins the emergence of Step Three peace. Sanity

A Heavenly Echo

is a sure sign of God's power working in our being, quite independent of our circumstances. We can have it by turning toward God in this Step. Who knows where the limits of this promise might be? But working the Steps will demonstrate that *deep assurance regardless of our trouble* becomes a working definition of sanity in these Steps. There are few things in life more certain or more blessed.

STEP THREE

Saying Yes to God

"We made a decision to turn our will and our lives over to the care of God as we understood God."

"But when he came to his senses, he said..., 'I will say..., "Father, I have sinned... in your sight; make me as one of your hired men."' And he got up and went to his father."

—LUKE 15:17–20

The Prodigal Son "came to himself" after hitting bottom in lonely hunger and misery in the "far country." Many since then have "bottomed" and begun the journey home in Steps One and Two. When exactly "home" is reached in the first three Steps is different for each individual. Somewhere in these Steps a light of lost reality happily comes on again. Where to begin among the many, many aspects of this perspective-changing transition? Dealing with false self-elevation must be among the first, whether we're listening to Bill W., Carl Jung, Jesus, or anyone, including "friends of Bill"! Jesus said, "Whoever exalts himself shall be humbled; and whoever humbles himself shall be exalted" (Matt. 23:12 NASB).

In discussing Steps One and Two we've noted that the world order gradually bears down on those who self-centeredly resist that life-supporting order. This leads to increasing unmanageability or powerlessness in our lives. Now we see the same principle from another perspective. Here, resisting nature's moral order takes the form of elevating oneself artificially, out of a fear of failure, weakness, or being "less than." This external approach to self-worth can be super competitive: it can be any driven effort to be seen as worthy of approval by vanquishing rather than loving our neighbors or seeking self-worth through God's care.

Turning our will and our life over to God's care is the absolute core of relating to God in this world. It is a decision, Step Three says, and a huge lifelong decision at that. It is one that we need God's help with the first time we do it and every time thereafter. The Step says, "We made a decision to turn over . . . ," not "We turned over . . ." This realism is consistent with all the thinking in the Steps. Step One says, "We admitted . . . ," indicating the *beginning* of making this decision; we move closer to it in Step Two with "We came to believe . . ."; and now we move closer still with "We made a decision"—a decisive act. We need help, not only in carrying this out throughout our lives, but at this very moment as we decide to turn ourselves over, to even initiate this blessed soul-motion toward God. We would find it unthinkably harder to make "a decision" such as this without the soul-shifts granted us in the movements of grace in Steps One and Two. And we couldn't even think of taking those first few steps if there were not already a connection between those steps and certain mystical, cosmic dynamics at work in our world.

In the Twelve Steps, Bill W. is writing by implication about a very different kind of universe than the one our present secularist culture urges us to believe in. At the very least, he had heard hymns like "The Battle Hymn of the Republic," which expresses this conflict of worldviews so effectively:

> He has sounded forth the trumpet that shall never call retreat;
> He is sifting out the hearts of men before His judgment seat.
> O be swift my soul to answer Him, be jubilant, my feet—
> Our God is marching on.

Though Bill W.'s Steps veil this poetic expression, they are equally providential in personal focus and effect. In Step Three, Bill W. is essentially saying that we answered God's gracious "sifting" in a decision that, aided by God's power (Step Two), resulted in a life of comparative jubilation. The first three Steps gradually persuaded us that God was present in them, acting on our souls in ways that made his care real and available to us—unconditionally (see Rom 8:38ff.). We came to believe a Power greater than our entire imagined selves. That Power began remaking our insane souls into sane ones, so much so that we began making a lifetime of decisions to trade in our control of life for his care. We were able to begin this life journey with a very limited understanding of God because of what the Steps made of that understanding. Only one thing mattered when we, like Bill W. and his friends, gave up on self-power and turned to a greater Power outside ourselves. It was that this quickly began to work as nothing else had.

In my nearly thirty years of working the Steps, I have increasingly seen that the authors were often filtering Christian messages through these principles. Step Three filters so many that it is hard to decide which to explore.

This may be a good time to comment on why the filtering became necessary. It can be argued that had the church in general maintained a healthy working out of its biblical principles, the AA program would not have been needed. All of the God- and self-relating principles of AA are clearly expressed in Jesus's teachings and those of his apostles. The 1930s AA movement filled a rather large vacuum where New Testament Christian teaching was only weakly affecting American culture. This situation still has not been remedied, and even many Christians today would agree.

I close this chapter with one last parallel between biblical and AA life principles. In the Apostle Paul's letter to the Romans, he says, "We know that in everything God works for the good of those who love God and are called according to His purpose" (8:28). In Step Three, Bill W. simply says that he and his friends decided to turn their lives over to God because they had seen enough of God's love proven to make that decision. We can only imagine, from our parallel recovery experience, the myriad attitude and thought changes—and serendipitous occurrences of "the good"—that these recovery pioneers went through. They came to know God's care as the most reliable dynamic in life through that dynamic recovery. They came to know that God works in all things for our good.

STEP FOUR

Living in the Light
Beginning Self-Acceptance and Self-Awareness

"We made a fearless and searching moral inventory of ourselves."

"Let a man examine himself, and so should he eat of the bread and drink of the cup."
—1 Corinthians 11:28

"First take the log out of your own eye, and then you will see . . . to take the speck out of your brother's eye."
—Matthew 7:5

Steps Four through Seven form a thematic sequence toward increasing consciousness and betterment of self. They move the soul toward taking account of our "defects of character," and into engaging God and other humans in removing "our shortcomings."

These ways of self-awareness and self-accountability are not surprising at all for the person who has recently discovered a wholly new and utterly trustworthy mode of self-validation. Paradoxically, when God, not self, is the source of worth, self's worth is greater. Recovering alcoholics come to know uniquely that God cares for them, having been decisively released from their hell. And when self's worth is genuinely greater, as an object of God's redeeming care, it can become aware of itself as a meaningful participant in God's plans for itself and others. Sharing life rather than survival of self takes a higher significance for God-saved persons.

This Step also springs rather naturally out of the new clarity about what the old, worthless self was up to in its behaviors. When those self-destructive choices were running the show, they seemed at least necessary, perhaps even right (which is wrong disguised as right). A worth-less self becomes increasingly delusional because of this bending of truth to fit its intense need. The reality of truth loses its clarity as it is habitually replaced with the needy self's shading of truth. The more the truth about the self's flaws is hidden, the less it can be restored. Police, therapists, and others encounter this every day. "The heart is deceitful above all things . . . who can know it?" (Jer. 17:9). The self that needs safety from improvement falsifies the books a lot.

The authors of the Big Book veered away from early childhood problems as the cause of their addictive traits. In fact, any kind of blame-shifting was suspect. They thought of their addictions as derived in part from allergies. Whether they actually derive largely from nature or nurture depends on who you talk to; regardless of your views on the science of it, it seems clear that most alcoholics have deeply embedded tendencies toward extremes of emotion and substance dependency.[1] Apparently, they have no less willpower or intelligence than most people, but they react to alcohol very poorly. The first three Steps help them accept their

---

1. Milt, *The Revised Basic Handbook on Alcoholism*, 131–35, and other chapters on AA in America.

"inbuilt" biological disadvantage, and there is no shame in needing this help. Paul, writing to the Romans, seems to raise the question of whether God uses inborn deficiencies so that his compassion will be shown in removing them (Rom 9:22–23). The result, then, is that no intelligent observer can miss God's involvement in the process. This is the gist of the Big Book writers' testimonies, and was the source of their motivation to improve their moral character. Newly washed souls are gratefully aware that they are in need of catching up morally, however they got behind.

Eventually, the main point for recovering alcoholics and for family members[2] is that the Steps program offers an effective present answer. Again, theories—religious or psychological—don't offer what turning from self to a Power greater than self offers. Self is not the answer for one in alcohol's grip, and this applies to the whole self. Thus the strong drive to make "a fearless and searching moral inventory of ourselves."

We will see how this principle attaches to the following self-searching Steps (Five, Six, and Seven). We will see why the authors, newly forming souls as they were, saw that such accuracy was so critical to staying sober.

---

2. See the affiliated organizations Al-Anon, Alateen, and Narcotics Anonymous (NA).

STEP FIVE

No Longer Alone

"We admitted to God, to ourselves, and to another human being the exact nature of our wrongs."

"Therefore confess your sins to one another."
—James 5:16

Years ago I heard a message by Juan Carlos Ortiz, an earnest Christian speaker who initiated a large renewal of Christianity in South America. In his talk at a friend's church, Ortiz said that very little of what Jesus's apostolic writers actually knew came through in the New Testament documents. Further, he said, very little of what came through in their writing has actually lodged in the minds of us who read them. This tells me that few individuals in history have heard God's message under circumstances dire enough to really, deeply register the power of his love. But many alcoholics have heard his love in precisely those desperate circumstances. AA's soul-changing phenomenon is how it frames God's message of love, spoken in life-or-death encounters, in the simplest terms. It is this: a heart painfully stripped of self-hope, merged with the simplified invitation, "Anyone who wants to be sober can join this company of faith in the God of your understanding."

There is a great deal more information in the gospel to absorb—which not all of us will agree on. Christians believe that it contains the entire God-driven scheme and energy for our world's creation. AA is a fantastically focused tool distilled from that meta-saga, with little of the Christian narrative but lots of its soul-quickening power. The AA mindset quickly evolved as a community and as individuals away from such religious complications.[1] Yet I think it's fair to observe that many positive developments of modernity, including science, were encouraged by Christian influence. Higher standards of living, social compassion, and movements such as AA were among those developments, despite the dilution and spoiling of the church in many ways.

In our era, we have observed a wealthy society living better materially than any other in history while accruing some of the same moral deficiencies as the rich ruling classes in our past. But when these bad moral attributes get going among the Judeo-Christian wealthy (as distinguished from the past pagan powerful), the distance penitents must travel to godly reform is shorter. Decadent, recovering alcoholics in our society have inherited an entire thesaurus of moral concepts that the Romans and many others never knew. Human life, for instance, had become much more valuable in society by the time Bill W. conceived of God and his moral duty to him.

Space does not allow us to explore the basic difference between ancient and medieval Western humanism and modernity under Christ's influence.[2] But I will note that the concept of self-betterment and loyalty to a benevolent God would have not formed part of Bill's total moral elevation had he lived in the Dark Ages rather than 1935. It's as though a huge psychological blanket

---

1. See *Twelve Steps and Twelve Traditions*.

2. See Lewis, *The Allegory of Love*. Lewis claims the very concept of love has fundamentally been raised to mean a warmer compassion.

had been lifted off the deep minds of those alcoholics, allowing the rise of a broad array of moral principles that had been in storage. A great morally revived community has arisen from this broadly supplied life-valuing perspective. From buried away in Bill's and his friends' deep minds under alcohol's anesthesia, there suddenly sprang one of the most vibrant examples of spiritual "repentance" in history. Called "penance" by many Jesus followers, it is one of the most basic human responses to God-awareness, impressively and naturally recovered out of the saved alcoholics' souls. The integrity of this "penance" is signaled by the admission of the exact nature of our wrongs to another human being. This kind of admission—or confession, to use the apostles' phrase—was more central to the community life of the first-century Christians. Those believers lived in close neighborhoods and were often as much family as church members—more so by a mile than our modern congregational type of church.[3]

When James directed these people to confess their sins to one another (Jas 5:16), it was not the problem it is now for us who are practically strangers. Alcoholics associate with each other much more like early house church members than we do in today's churches; they know each other's "wrongs" rather graphically, and avoiding this part of themselves is certain failure for their sobriety. Indeed, they have much more to gain from such admission than church congregants in general. Here and there among Evangelical or Pentecostal groups and others, "accountability" has endured historically to some extent, or taken root anew. But it is rarely a robust practice of community as it was in Christianity's first movements, or as it is in the integrity of the current twelve-step family.

May the freedom and cleansing of Step Five appeal to each soul who reads of it, whether here or in AA. For any addict attempting to walk through all Twelve Steps, it will become readily apparent at Step Nine and in others that involve human relationships whether Steps Four through Seven were processed. One can't make amends if his or her ego hasn't faced the false justification of self-ignorance and denial in the earlier Steps. Only when we

---

3. Banks, *Paul's Idea of Community*.

humbly accept ourselves and seek improvement can we take responsibility toward those we have wounded and talk with them. The Steps are in the right order, and they will take you where you need to be.

In *Abba's Child*, Brennan Manning quotes psychiatrist James Knight regarding alcoholics: "These persons have had their lives laid bare and pushed to the brink of destruction by alcoholism. . . . When these persons arise from the ashes of the hellfire of addictive bondage, they have an understanding . . . and willingness to enter into and maintain healing encounters with their fellow alcoholics. In this encounter they cannot and will not permit themselves to forget their brokenness and vulnerability. Their wounds are acknowledged . . . and kept visible. Further, their wounds are used to *illuminate* and stabilize their own lives. . . . The effectiveness of AA's members . . . is one of the great success stories of our time."[4]

---

4. Manning, *Abba's Child*, 26.

STEP SIX

Deep Desire for God's Influence

"We were entirely ready to have God remove all these defects of character."

"But the tax-gatherer... unwilling to lift up his eyes to heaven, was beating his breast, saying, God be merciful to me, a sinner."

—Luke 18:13

This great Step takes us into the very heart of the human being's potential desire for God's kingdom and right character. The Mosaic covenant commanded at the beginning of the law that each of us should love the Lord our God with all our powers ("mind, soul, strength"). Jesus said, in urging our priorities Godward, "Seek first His kingdom and righteousness and all these things will be added to you" (Matt 6:33).

But these biblical directives express God's moral precepts, which are frequently out of reach for you and me and our recovering brothers and sisters. These middle Steps cannot be interpreted

DEEP DESIRE FOR GOD'S INFLUENCE

to contradict Steps One through Three, which speak of God's gracious power to grant sanity and supernatural care in our worst weakness. Step Six conforms to this God-oriented grace, but even in aiming directly at "removing these defects of character," we must be clear that this is not a reversion to self-righteousness. Moses and Jesus speak of what each of us *should* be doing toward God. But this emphasis must be balanced with the Step Six words, "ready to have God remove all these defects." When I say that this great Step takes us into the human being's potential desire for God's right character, I am pressing on one side of the central dilemma of God-human relationship. This side shows humans wanting to be more like God, to improve themselves morally. The other side of the dilemma shows us largely unable to live up to our desire. Paul devoted quite a bit of space to confessing this reality in his letter to the Romans (7:14–25). There he concludes, "The wishing is present in me, but the doing of the good is not" (v. 18). The apostle (who authored much of the New Testament) is referring to the very law of God-human relations that commands primary devotion to God and high morality toward our neighbors. This is the law that all people routinely fail to fulfill. He says here that he cannot keep it perfectly either, though he greatly desires to.

We are discussing Step Six—a Step preparing our minds for repentance from Godless living. Yet we are also of necessity discussing the Christian idea of salvation by faith, the screened-out backdrop of AA redemption. This Christian concept is taught splendidly in the first eight chapters of that Roman epistle. It is a radical advance in the ways an infinitely righteous Creator and a deeply imperfect humanity can be reconciled. This marvelous solution can be summed up thus: Christ died for all men, and God now declares all men dead in his death and alive, as God's gift, in his resurrection. This word "gift," from the Greek *charis*, grants eternal life to all who will truly accept it. Paul spends many paragraphs illustrating how God planned and executed this salvation for his world. He emphasizes God's grace so much that critics then and since have accused him of a cheap, no-effort gospel, requiring an explanation for this radical idea. In Romans 6:1 he must answer their question: "Are we to continue in sin that grace might increase?" His rather lengthy reply to this question is, again, only summarized here: how can anyone who has experienced the joyous release from sin in Christ want to return to the previous existence? The apostle is saying that many humans want to live better, but they find it hard to do, and his moral relativism allows hope.

"Relativism" must be quickly clarified. Here is the essential Christian paradox: attempts to live a perfect life are bound to fail because our spiritual constitution cannot support it. Moral law grimly acquaints us with this sad fact of human life. We must have love from the only perfect One as an unconditional gift, as something not of ourselves. This language begins to sound similar to the wonderful grace insights that the first three Steps express. To paraphrase, Step One says, "I can't"; Step Two, "God can"; Step Three, "I receive his gift of care." The Steps also reflect other language from Paul's gospel—for instance, in Romans 6:19: "For just as you presented your members as slaves to impurity . . . so now present [them] as slaves to righteousness."

Addiction-enslaved alcoholics who work the Steps know this wondrous release, and they know uniquely that they depend on God's power as the determiner of their new walk. Thus each serious Twelve Stepper realizes that he or she has turned in one kind of master for another—one leading to death and the other to life. Many recoverees have said that they've turned in a sick compulsion for a healthier one, and the essence of Step Six echoes that dependence: "to have God remove all these defects." In the same breath, they repeatedly express their belief that they are not perfect. They are just happier—and therefore better—humans.

Again and again the Steps reflect grace rather than moralism. Yes, there must be a moral guide, but the power is in love. Law is like a physician's diagnosis, grace-love like the healing prescription.

The paradox in both Christianity and the Twelve Steps is that *relief from law's deadly consequences moves the human spirit to live out God's will better than if someone must fulfill it in order to be valued and accepted.* This is the moral relativism, or grace's relief from the law's strict penalty, mentioned a few paragraphs earlier.

Deep Desire for God's Influence

The gospel and the Steps are greatly about the heart, its motivation and trust. The heart's desire will always be more encouraged by a love Power greater than itself.

Thus the language of these Steps reflects human minds that knew God's inexpressible, addiction-delivering love-power for them. Their hope to be better men had taken flight. They saw God's love transform severely sick, even dying, persons—often with their wide-eyed participation. And if God could remove the irresistible urge to drink, why could he not also remove enough defects of character in one's soul that others would take note and benefit? Gain, not perfection, was the emphasis.

Few people know better than recovering alcoholics that they are not perfect, nor God.

STEP SEVEN

Walking the Talk, by Faith

"We humbly asked Him to remove our shortcomings."

"But one thing I do, forgetting what lies behind, and reaching forward
. . . I press on toward the goal . . . of the upward call of God."

—Philippians 3:13–14

We have been climbing incrementally up the mountain of God since Step Four, preparing in each Step for this life-altering petition to God. Who can fail to notice the meticulous, thoughtful care that the Steps devote to parsing out this approach to God?

From the stupendous release of Step Three to the audacious Step Seven petition, we have covered a lot of spiritual ground. We've seen thorough self-examination (Step Four), excruciatingly naked moral admission (Step Five), and deep-soul spiritual repentance (Step Six). In all of the Twelve Steps, no other sequence of Steps is so written through with God's Spirit. God's gracious encouragement leads us here, to where the mind is prepared by the unction of the Spirit to be under his influence by faith.

I do not hide the fact that Christian terminology is creeping in here, yet I find it appropriate, for this is a faith petition. Jesus said, "Ask and it shall be given to you." (Matt 7:7). In the early Communist era, a Chinese Christian, Watchman Nee, wrote a book called *The Normal Christian Life*. In this book Nee asserts that there is a fabulously rich and real relationship attainable in Christ that many Christians do not experience; he says this is the normal life for believers. Bearing witness to this is the fact that Nee and his wife, though separated in Chinese prison camps, faced their deaths with remarkable serenity. Analogous to this experience, Bill W. and his spiritual companions were "walking the walk" through these Steps, a walk parallel to the "normal" life God seeks for those he is redeeming from their hell. Their "walk" language reveals this: that they increasingly came to see and value life as it was emptied of soul-barriers to God's direction.

The life-altering petition in this Step is relational to the core: God is asked to act on my soul to cleanse and mold it by his dynamic being. This reminds us of the Prophet Isaiah's invitation, "Come, let us reason together, though your sins be as scarlet, they will be as . . . snow" (1:18). And King David's famous prayer fits here also: "Create in me a clean heart, O God, and renew a right spirit within me. . . . The sacrifices of God are a broken spirit, a broken and a contrite heart" (Ps 51:10,17).

The approach to the Step Seven prayer echoes this kind of change of heart meticulously, particularly in Step Six's declaration, "We were entirely ready to have God remove all these defects." This is God-inspiration very like that evidenced in Isaiah's, David's, and others' responses to God. From Genesis to Revelation, we humans are said to be in God's image; this Step describes the deep-seated longing that our God-nature provokes. God is love, John wrote, and his image in us stirs us to improve ourselves as our defects impact those we love. Step Six lies right at the door of Steps Eight and Nine, which will issue in the most rational follow-up to the soul-cleansing, love-increasing power of Step Seven.

Step Seven, in its expressed desire to improve spiritually, to have more of the image of God within, is linked to the Genesis story of man's first longing toward God. There in chapters 2 and 3, Adam and Eve are seen immensely enjoying intimate union with their Maker in the cool of each day—also translated the wind, the stirring, of each day—and by implication, longing to be more like him. They were created for this (Gen 2:15ff.; 3:8). That natural desire to become more like one's mentor or superior was soon to become an overpowering sense of impossibility and moral failure (Gen 3:10ff.). Now the longing to become better, to emulate their great model, had expanded into a crushing gap between their "naked" weakness and their God's glorious spiritual beauty. This is the Genesis vision of the source of human despair. Self-defending and self-deceiving reactions to God's beauty fill so much of human history. Bill W. and his friends confessed that it was these false, self-expanding reactions that had driven them to the end of their rope. God's caring power for sobriety lay waiting there.

And here in Steps Four through Seven we see a recovery of that original, creation-driven longing and hope to be more like our Maker. In *Made for Heaven*, a little book on heaven's character, C. S. Lewis declares that this is the great human longing, which heaven above all else fulfills.[1] He says that foretastes of this fulfillment are part of true Christian experience in the present life. This, he says, is why teaching on heaven matters and why he is writing of it.

Here Bill W. and friends agree in principle if not in explicit verbal doctrine. In other words, these AA pioneers experienced foretastes of divine life in deliverance from their hell and in their spiritual awakening.

This new spiritual consciousness not only put in them the power to escape their deadly addictions—it also kindled in them the desire to be better men than they had been. They placed a higher value on all creation than they did before. They were more a part of God than before, and more a part of other humans.

---

1. Lewis, *Made for Heaven*, 70ff.

Walking the Talk, by Faith

The moment God touched them with power over addiction, they began to hope again that it was all true: that God had made them to serve his great purposes in the world, so that their little lives, though small, mattered. They aimed at this life goal because whether they succeeded or not, it was worth everything to aim at it with their whole strength.

STEP EIGHT

Developing a Conscience

"We made a list of all persons we had harmed, and became willing to make amends to them all."

The new pattern of living that Steps Eight through Ten introduce comes somewhat naturally to the newly spiritually minded individual. Awareness or consciousness is the key dynamic, as we have discussed earlier. In *The Message: The Bible in Contemporary Language*, Eugene Peterson paraphrases Jesus's teaching about this from Matthew 13:13ff. Jesus was telling stories (parables) that day, and in explaining this teaching method said, "Whenever someone has a heart ready for this, the insights and understandings flow freely" (MSG). This heart-readiness is evidence of the new birth and life that both the first Twelve Steppers and the earliest Christians testified to so passionately. When a human soul comes alive spiritually, it—like any living thing—will grow, and these spiritual Steps show the nature of spiritual growth. Jesus made numerous statements to the effect that "the insights flow freely" when the heart is ready for love and joy and hope. Someone has said of

Developing a Conscience

Judaism's earlier contributions to human progress also that love is the highest form of knowledge.

Love was the heart energy that built the humanity of the early AA pioneers; we see it continually throughout Steps Four through Ten. To heal wounds in those we've hurt becomes a natural impulse in the spiritually quickened mind. Our conscience grows in strength as we experience God's gracious treatment in the face of our "wrongs" and "defects." "He that is forgiven much loves much," Jesus observed (Luke 7:47), and Steps Eight through Ten loudly echo this wonderful characteristic of the God-birthed human heart. No one is as grateful for heaven as those saved out of hell, and so we become "willing to make amends to them all."

STEP NINE

Developing Skill in Relationships

"We made direct amends to such people wherever possible, except when to do so would injure them or others."

It is a challenging spiritual exercise to return to "the scene of the crime" in our amends making. It is an exercise that provides experience and perspective in the relational aspect of being human—which forms at least 90 percent of our humanness. After proceeding through Step Nine, many recoverees begin to see that being wrong (and often) is more normal than they once thought. Some begin to trade in the goal of being consistently "right" toward others for the goal of affecting others positively as much as possible.

One of the happy consequences of amends making is the frequent reconciliations, large and small, between offenders and offended. They help normalize humility. Years ago I gently confronted an influential twelve-step leader about his insensitivity after being put off by him earlier. He immediately became still and said, "You're right; that was not considerate of me. I could improve on that." Later I wrote him a note of appreciation for his maturity

Developing Skill in Relationships

in acknowledging the wrong, communicating my respect for him and the encouragement I had received from his act of honest humility. This interaction proved valuable for both of us. Step Ten was obviously part of his life.

"Making amends" as a theme could fill many volumes, with its relational value and the difficulties and disappointments it entails. In Step Ten we can see "normal" as including the ongoing readiness to admit our "wrongs." I am writing about Steps 9 and 10 almost interchangeably (and Step 8 also a little), which seems rather natural; I will now include a necessary observation on perfectionism in Step 10. However, as we see in the next Step, this heart-readiness can also be overemphasized.

STEP TEN

Ongoing Self-Acceptance and Perfectionism

"We continued to take personal inventory and when wrong, promptly admitted it."

All the Steps require the repeated use of Steps One through Three: we are constantly facing our powerlessness, turning to God's power, and surrendering ourselves to his care. Without this ongoing self-dying, we cannot live with what we are—in the tension of longing to be good in ways that we know we are not. Or good in ways that we have forgotten we are not. Steps Four through Ten can be carefully applied to our current relationships in ways that increase self-awareness. Steps Eight through Ten especially are about conscious, loving relationships that build secure trust and bonding and good boundaries. (This is most crucial and often most difficult among family members.) The Serenity Prayer illuminates this struggle poignantly: "God, grant me the serenity to accept the things I cannot change, the courage to change the things I can, and the wisdom to know the difference." Here,

Ongoing Self-Acceptance and Perfectionism

serenity in the struggle for self-awareness and acceptance can give us peace with reality: we don't see ourselves quite perfectly; we are "normal" this way (many Adult Children struggle here); we don't have to be wonderful or superior to be acceptable.

With respect to self-knowledge, it is better to know you don't know than to think you do when you don't. Part of serenity is simply accepting that you are not and do not need to be exceptional, perfect, or near perfect. Discovering "wrong" in your behavior from time to time is just part of this humanness. Deflation, a word used in the early Step descriptions, applies well here.

I must add to all this an observation from ongoing recovery life: I must avoid the tendency to idealize recovery—a common, often unconscious temptation for many of us in recovery. I suspect that perfectionism is a real enemy of healthy relating for many of the millions of AA recoverees and affected family members. The yearning for everything to be alright bears down on addictive family members; in fact, it acts in most humans with developing consciences. To take up moral responsibility and still accept oneself as far from fully moral is one of the great burdens of the religious mind. This is why grace and unconditional love are such powerful motivators for humans. Stumbling must be an acceptable part of learning to walk.

Paradoxically, as I have noted above, we are more relaxed and genuinely caring with those we love when we consciously accept our relational imperfection. In *Adult Children of Alcoholics*, Janet Woititz emphasizes that guilt does no good for injured loved ones, nor for us injurers. She gives guidelines for how to enhance recovery and offers practical hope that much of this pain is reversible.[1]

I include this discussion of perfectionism (and its denial) here in order to balance out my more optimistic talk of relational possibilities in Steps Eight through Ten. Recovering people's struggles with marriage, family, friendships, and vocation seem to be on par with those of their non-addictive neighbors. This observation doesn't come from comprehensive study but simply from my reading, acquaintance with others, and my own struggles. Needing and

---

1. Woititz, *Adult Children of Alcoholics*, chap. 4.

using the Steps gives us recoverees some amazing insights about our human nature, and a sometimes joyful, self-accepting humility about needing help; but in the end, we should consider ourselves lucky just to return to the fold of ordinary humanity by means of that help. Expecting much more than this from "walking the walk" should be a red flag pointing to the kind of thinking that started all our troubles in the first place.

STEP ELEVEN

Growing God-Consciousness, Seeking the Impossible

"We sought through prayer and meditation to improve our conscious contact with God as we understood Him, praying only for knowledge of His will for us and the power to carry that out."

"Our Father who art in Heaven, hallowed by Thy name. Thy kingdom come, Thy will be done, on earth as it is in heaven. Give us this day our daily bread, and forgive us our debts as we forgive our debtors. Lead us not into temptation, but deliver us from evil."

—Matthew 6:9

Here again the Steps turn Godward, circling back in Steps Eleven and Twelve to themes like those in the first three. These last two Steps are also linked interdependently and work in parallel: the first part of both Eleven and Twelve is about directly relating to God through prayer, meditation, and spiritual awakening; the second part is about human-level relating by carrying out God's will, sharing this message with other addicts, and practicing these principles continually.

Both the spiritual awakening and the cultivation of a prayer life with a living God-power appear to have a developmental quality. They are mentioned in the last two Steps, and this placement probably reflects the fact that sobriety (and transformation) is generally a gradual, educational process. Many addicts report that this was their experience of achieving sobriety, while for some it was more sudden and dramatic.

One of the beautiful developments we see in the stories of Bill W. and his friends, stories of life regained, is the restoration of spirituality. Yes, it all seems "new," and the power and perspective clearly are—but some other aspects of this clean and sober life have a familiar ring to them. These reborn individuals seemed to have an inner library of God-knowledge. This morality was readily accessible to their conscious mind once they began shifting away from self-as-solution to "a Power greater" than themselves. This accessible spiritual-relational library continually supplied them with principles of better responsibility for their souls' moral character. Their behavior toward others, as well as toward "God" (as they understood him), was improved. However, before this awakening, they had been quite familiar with the Golden Rule and morality in the traditional sense—though their lives belied this knowledge. They knew the Ten Commandments and all such standards, and resources for meditation were everywhere. Prayer and meditation were intuitive concepts to most of them, as was moral responsibility. So it was not simply new knowledge that they needed before they could change. It was something more.

The experience that the authors of the Steps narrate seems to affirm the idea that until we awaken spiritually—and even afterward, only to a lesser degree—we humans know more than we perform morally and spiritually. The self holds sway until some provocation occurs to turn us from self to God as life's determiner. The actual "spirits" involved in addiction represent the

Growing God-Consciousness, Seeking the Impossible

self-centered perception toward life that "the god of this world" perpetuates.

This spirit is real and can dominate a person's entire mentality through alcohol. Bill's friends found its dominance broken only by the power of the real God. Once they felt the amazing inner release that simply turning to God provided, they quickly saw the deceit they had existed under previously. Their new minds were now creatively compliant with much of what the best of religion and philosophy had offered all along.

All the spiritual dynamics involved in relating happily to other people, to self, and to God operate continually and everywhere in our world. Once we perceive God as a friend capable of delivering us from alcohol's deadly power, all these intuitive interactions begin rising to consciousness. Learning about our faults is necessary, and this new life-consciousness helps us do so. Also necessary is learning about the feelings of others and the majesty of the greater Power who delivers from alcohol's prison.

Step Eleven insightfully expresses a purity of motive in prayer—"praying only for knowledge of His will for us and the power to carry that out." This way of seeing the purpose of prayer stems from Step Three and the decision "to turn our will and our lives over to the care of God." Turning everything over to God shifts the central purpose of one's existence, one decision at a time, from self-gain and self-determination to God's will. This shift occurs when one's life is in ruins, and nothing is the same again after that ruinous power is broken by the quiet inner decision to turn oneself over to God. Nothing is the same with the resource of prayer: friendship, family, vocation, success, status, mortality, everything is changed. The addict's inner mind now responds to fear from within the safety of a bond with God, one that has been proven by his release from hell. Prayer is now about relating appropriately to God, not getting something for self. Self no longer carries the same importance in existence that it once did; it will never again be trusted as a source of well-being compared to God. Learning life and loving grow in importance; our conscious contact with God improves. There is much to meditate on in our daily experience from this point of view, because every experience, whether ordinary or extraordinary, seems to be an opportunity for becoming a better human and understanding God more. God is a friendly concept now, and encouragement appears regularly in all kinds of wisdom, conversations, and events. This is a happy Step and reveals a lot about what life was once headed toward in pain and loss. This is all compared to now, in which our self is just part of something large and freeing and happily purposeful. The addict now depends upon God, not "the spirits," and is happy cooperating, continually seeing the reality of God's power working to carry out his will.

But we should not proceed to the last Step without a comment on the less happy side of "learning and loving" in our conscious contact with God. I'm afraid I've made it sound too easy when, in fact, old habits die hard. Other Steppers and I have had to develop a daily structure to keep ourselves conscious in our "conscious contact." Something like the following has helped us greatly; it is not unlike spiritual exercises among religiously disciplined people. I call it "Preview and Review," a daily use of the first three Steps in the morning (Preview) and again in the evening at day's close (Review). Review comes more naturally to us, since the day brings unexpected incidents and it is often only in hindsight that we realize we should have used the Steps at those moments. Preview can be added to set our minds up better preemptively, to walk in a more surrendered and trusting attitude through the day's irregularities and challenges. By God's grace, second chances (Review) are abundantly available and helpful. But we can add to our conditioned peace of mind by the Preview use of these principles.

STEP TWELVE

Amazing Grace
Knowing and Sharing Our God-Life

"Having had a spiritual awakening as a result of these Steps, we tried to carry this message to alcoholics and to practice these principles in all our affairs."

"But we all . . . beholding as in a mirror the glory of the Lord, are being transformed into the same image from glory to glory, just as from the Lord, the Spirit."
—2 Corinthians 3:18

"Blessed are the pure in heart, for they shall see God."
—Matthew 5:8

One of the early converts to the twelve-step life said that he began it simply seeking sobriety but ended up finding God.

A Heavenly Echo

Many recovering alcoholics reported the warm and wonderful brotherhood they experienced in the growing twelve-step meetings and social gatherings. A whole new life opened up to many of them. They were happily awake to God's powerful, saving care and to the inexpressible joy of seeing other addicts successfully join this saving community. They had had "spiritual awakening," which meant they experienced God in a new light—what they called a "vital spiritual experience." They became "addicted" to bringing other alcoholics to this life, and were driven to practice these principles in every part of their lives.

The developmental, educational pattern of AA tells us that every part of their lives and relationships were involved—body, soul, and spirit. This also involved their relationship with self, God, and society. One can imagine hearing the echoes of their recovery song in many familiar Step phrases all through the Steps, "admitted," "came to believe," "sanity," "turned over to God's care," "self-inventory," "made amends" to others, practiced "admitting" wrongs . . . These words signify signposts on a new road "less traveled," one that they were moved powerfully to take and had consciously decided to take. On the one hand, a present greater Power; on the other, their decision—free beings, one infinite and one finite, both capable of the most complex process in conscious existence: the process of choosing to whom to give oneself and from whom to withhold. Autonomy is a widespread feature in nature and human beings, a wonderful and high-risk gift. I will say more about it soon in connection with man's unique giftedness in his power to recognize his Maker here and in eternity.

The finite chooser lives contingently in a three-dimensional time-space bubble. Here the Infinite One has entered by descending even to the finite surrender-point of our death. Here in our world, our very limited perception is met by a host of time-space symbols created in nature and society by this Incarnate One. From this we begin to apprehend that we are loved and can be contacted, helped, and changed positively by this Power's intervention. Some of these time-space symbols include nature's splendor and grandeur, family love, morality, conscience and consciousness, the gospel of a resurrected God-man, death, and yes, pain and pleasure. All of these phenomena are either part of the natural order or relayed to us in it by human witnesses. But from Jesus's resurrection we deduce that they all reflect a larger, invisible order.

Other, better theologians and writers have admitted that the reasons are murky for our being made in a world in which we can see so little of this Infinite One. But certainly the fact that we can see only his choice-inducing influence, not his absolute power, makes our free choosing of God more genuine. The Infinite One's choice to limit himself, the most extreme end of which is his suffering with and within our world, poignantly answers the suffering and evil that form such a significant part of his creation. It also tinges with hope our questions about the character and purposes of such a God in creating.

One of the best, most down-to-earth answers to such questions is found in the record of these twelve-step pioneers, and in the life-redeeming principle they discovered and lived. It has to do with the unique Creator-to-created choosing that we have introduced above. Their record shows just how life-giving this choosing can be.

Through their life-restoring experience with this mysterious, variously symbolized Power, Bill and his friends "came to believe" that they had a vital connection with this One. What to call him became far less important than what he did for them when they believed. It meant immeasurable freedom when they realized that any way they understood him was good enough to lead them out of their hell; the door opened to another side of reality with this marvelous release from misery and theological gamesmanship. Help was not reserved for the religiously informed. Their ignorance of religion was simply not an issue with this Power. All that was needed was a real desire to turn from self to God as the source of healing.

Once they made this inner move and alcohol began to lose its grip, they knew who was truly God in this world. Then the Twelve Steps took them deeper into life—they experienced cleansing change of their true motives, defects, and how they understood themselves and God. Prayer became a vital part of this gradual spiritual awakening. Some of them truly felt in their deepest hearts that they had been "born again." Many who said they had resented Christian clergy and their sermonizing began to relax their views, thinking that maybe the clergy had been right on the main ideas all along. Many others were quite happy with those members of AA who chose to participate in church life. "Live and let live" was their new, positive, more confident outlook.

When I, as a clergyman myself, first began to view this AA history in 1987, I remember thinking that this new charity in the Steppers toward self and others was a reflection of the kingdom of God in them. This new charity was both engaged with and fed by serving others, especially other addicts. The thrilling, joyful satisfaction of connecting with other alcoholics and seeing them come back to life was often equal to the gladness of their own sobriety. One such reborn alcoholic writes in the Big Book, "I hope I have been able to impart to you, the reader, at least a bit of what I know, the joy of living, the irresistible power of divine love and its healing strength, and the fact that we as sentient beings, have the knowledge to choose between good and evil, and choosing good, are made happy."[1] Over and over again, recovering alcoholics wrote or spoke of the immense gratification they received not only from gaining sobriety but also from helping someone else attain it.

I cannot help but notice the universality of the principle at work here. It is at work among all individuals who experience a new birth of God's Spirit in faith. The new life expresses itself in self-reproduction. This beautiful sharing spirit has driven many missions of gospel mercy and sacrifice in Christ's people. However, spirituality is not the only dynamic energy that exhibits this reaching out from self; it is seen in all that is alive in any way in the Creator's world—in plants, animals, and human love, and in the energy cycles of nature, micro and macro.

It is very beautiful to see a human soul receive such happy, rich fulfillment from successfully sharing this life-healing power with another. The one who shares has intimate knowledge of what

---

1. Bill W., *Alcoholics Anonymous*, 543.

joy is occurring in the new convert; the two are one in a life-reproducing moment. They experience powerfully what we all yearn to know: that we humans are all connected meaningfully. And that we are all connected to God.

The Twelfth Step's report of a "spiritual awakening as a result of these steps" shows the interconnectedness of the twelve, especially of the first three. We can also see that everything following Step Three depends upon that step. The stories from the AA book show that after a person experienced the release of sobriety by turning over his or her will to God, the rest of the Steps fell rationally into place. They had much to learn in this walk. But self-inventory and correction, amends to others, prayer, sharing, sobriety, and living out this more "self-less" life pattern became meaningful and fulfilling aspects of sobriety, and of life. They began to know something good about God and about living that they had once considered an infringement on the rights of self. They became connected to God, to themselves, and to other human beings (Step Five) in positive, caring ways. But it all began in Steps One through Three—by turning from self to God as the center of life.

In Step Twelve the authors are saying that because of Steps One through Eleven, they woke up spiritually, spent much of their lives sharing this new life with alcoholics, and consciously incorporated these principles in every part of their lives. AA is not about sobriety alone; it is about a spiritually directed way of living happily as a human in the world.

Soon after my middle child's introduction to AA (in Al Anon), he shared something along these lines with me. When he started with Al Anon, he was thinking he would use this "tool" to fix his life and then get into the normal life again. A few weeks later, however, as he told me enthusiastically, he had come to the realization that he was actually taking up a whole new way of living, of seeing himself, others, and God. He was seeing that he would both need and enjoy this way for the rest of his natural life. He was no longer the center of life, and its management from now on was in the hands of a much greater Power.

This brings us quite naturally to one of the other great life-building precepts shared by the gospel and the AA walk: that of sanctification, or individuation—in the language of faith and psychology, respectively. We are separating from our old life and building a new one, a new, specific image of God in our personality. A regularly repeated variation of this truth as a prayer can aid our development. We can keep asking God to separate us from our old life and to put the God-inspired version of a new, sanctified soul in place of our old one.

This deflated view of the self is where all AA's unique traditions and its enduring and growing organizational life came from. Well-known AA organizational descriptions such as "autonomy," "attraction," "not promotion," and "live-and-let-live" sing among many choral and orchestral marching tunes, leading many out of the cacophony of a self-trapped, desperately seeking world.

POSTSCRIPT

Humanity beyond Sobriety, Time-Space, and Death

The main purpose of this brief essay is to not only show agreement between the Twelve Steps and the gospel but to make clear the startling spiritual uniqueness of that gospel. Distinguished from its garbled Christian history, the gospel can be seen as sharply focused, like the Steps, on the power of God's love to restore the human soul. In the gospel saga of God suffering (and resurrected) with our world through his Son, many in human history have experienced this power, centered in Jesus's terrible death for them.

Students of the Twelve Steps practice and enjoy that life-transforming power; they and others increasingly study its psycho-spiritual dynamics. The same response developed among earlier and later witnesses to the power of Jesus's death and resurrection.

Dr. John Polkinghorne, a physicist-turned-theologian, writes that the later Christian witnesses (third century AD) began to ponder the meaning of Jesus's death and resurrection much like early twentieth-century physicists pondered the shocking implications of quantum physics.[1] The universe these physicists perceived

---

1. Polkinghorne, *The God of Hope and the End of the World*, 17ff.

in their discoveries was quite different from the one they had previously understood. These discoveries included a great deal of consciousness-reflecting and producing character. In the same way, the earliest Christian witnesses and the twelve-step pioneers were overwhelmed by the impact of their discoveries, which had transformed their lives. Only later did all three communities ask, "What has happened?" Something highly unexpected from the natural order happened in Judea in AD 30, in alcohol-plagued America in the 1930s, and in the first years of twentieth-century physics in the Western world. Each of these areas of historic discovery suggests a mysterious reality beyond our natural universe. "What has happened?" indeed—in each case that question will keep humanity searching in earnest for a long, long time.

I propose that we look briefly but deeply into the story of the power of this gospel event, this "happening," in the hope that now is a time when all can do so. From this reflection I hope we can catch a glimpse of our world's eternal origin and purpose. In any case, this is one perspective on it all from a Christian twelve-step student who believes that all these things are from the same Power.

The gospel story says, in brief, that long ago humankind lost vital contact with God, resulting in tragic, deadly consequences. Jesus's appearance in our world is the gift of God's actual presence among us, to restore that contact in our own form. It is the true perception of this sacrificially loving God that changes us and makes us like him (1 John 3:2). In the present world this is called faith; in the next it will be directly observed heavenly reality. John states in one verse the whole character of the gospel's hope of our eternal existence: we will be like God "*because* we will see [perceive] Him exactly as He is." This kind of "seeing" has the power to transform our souls into God-like souls forever. This is not because of our good character but simply out of our capacity to appreciate God's. Bill W. and his cohorts saw or knew in a new, immediate way the God they had only heard of as he broke alcohol's power over them. This seeing of God's power changed the way they saw everything—and themselves. They were new men. This was the vision of our life that Jesus shared in John 3:5: "Unless a man is born of . . . the

Humanity Beyond Sobriety, Time-Space, and Death

Spirit, he cannot enter [see] the kingdom of God." It is the same new life character his apostle Paul wrote about in 2 Corinthians 5:17: "If any person is in Christ, he is a new creature."

This new birth of our spirit is God's gift, as is the new perception of God that comes with it. It is out of this new God-perception that a new, God-like soul begins to emerge. As an addict or child of an addict freed from alcohol's hell sees this greater Power able to care for him in sobriety, he knows that this Power is truly God. According to the Bible, this kind of knowing is precisely what humans are made for—"to worship God and enjoy him forever." Great Christians articulated this long ago. This spiritual core fact of existence is fabulous news for addicts and their families. It is *gospel*, good news, for any individual who now "humbly asks" God for his care, because it means a radically freeing and hopeful shift in the fundamental character of how we relate to God.

Before, most of us thought this relationship depended upon our being a person of good character, keeping the rules decently, and so on. Now it means essentially a deep inner knowledge of God, a startling recognition of his absolutely unconditional care for us. Nothing else that we might perceive about our most secret soul or about human history or about society tops this. Arriving with blessed sobriety and with our decision to turn over our lives to God's care simultaneously, this liberating knowledge rapidly forms an unbreakable bond of trust with our Creator. "I found God" certainly means "I see Him, I get it!"—and nothing could mean more. This life-quickening, transforming perception of God follows a long line of faith testimony that was filtered, perhaps unconsciously, through the twelve-step people's minds. The Apostle Paul saw this in a similar grace encounter with the risen Jesus (see Acts 9:1–6, the account of Paul's dramatic vision). Much later he wrote from his years of following this Christ, "For I am convinced that neither death, nor life, nor angels, nor principalities, nor things present, nor things to come, nor powers, nor height, nor depth, nor anything in existence shall be able to separate us from the love of God, which is in Christ Jesus" (Rom 8:38–39).

A Heavenly Echo

I referred above to Jesus's resurrection as the unique spiritual foundation of the belief that human life is just beginning in the present time. Christ's life indicates that much, much more awaits us beyond our sight in eternity. This is the cornerstone of historic Christian faith, and it interlocks with God's certain saving power in this world, where alcoholics "get it." These two themes fit together beatifically: being saved so convincingly here in time, and perceiving that this new life experience foretells the character of our eternal existence with God.

Again, Jesus's great apostle Paul wrote enticingly of that still-invisible reality: "Things which eye has not seen and ear has not heard, and which have not entered the heart of man, all that God has prepared for those who love Him" (1 Cor 2:9). In another place he wrote that the sufferings of this life do not even compare to the glory that is to follow (Rom 8:18). These visionary expressions, along with the statement in 1 John that we will see God as he actually is, portray a life to come in which humans will occupy a deeply important role, one that could even be called ecstatic: being members of God's eternal family.

The great point for the here and now is that the AA program and the gospel share an experience of God-reality that is truly life-changing and extraordinarily exciting. The problem is that "Christianity" has clouded its marvelous message with partisanship internally and political oppression externally. This has often muted the very best and most exhilarating parts of its message. By setting the heart of the gospel alongside the twelve-step program, we see that the gospel, which has historically been muted, is in reality as life-lifting here and now as the Steps when it is understood and lived; and it holds out a uniquely magnificent vision of humanity's heritage with God beyond this life.

It is my purpose to state these enthralling Christian precepts here. My hope is that the renewed, clean, and sober individual might be able to recognize and accept them when they are separated from their historical baggage. The gospel, since it has common ground with AA precepts, elevates one's present walk and gives a mind-boggling view of the future in eternity.

Humanity beyond Sobriety, Time-Space, and Death

The actual Christian saga, the core gospel in the apostolic writings, is that Jesus was God as well as man, and that his death and resurrection in the early first century reunited the human race with God. This reuniting, says the gospel, has made every human acceptable to God again forever; this is a gift available to all who recognize the lack of humanity in themselves and who will sincerely receive the gift. Receiving it literally joins one to Christ and to his Body—his church, or those who are "gathered." The gospel says further that this Body is the first level of God's re-creation of all humankind and nature, and the whole cosmos. This cosmic rejuvenation will also affect heavenly entities in ways that set an eternally insurmountable barrier between our heavenly existence and sin or death. We are guaranteed eternal blissful existence.

Whether or not this grand, wonderful time-and-eternity vision is true is not the point of this discussion. Volumes have been written to establish its veracity and to deny it. The idea here is to understand it, to see what it is that has driven Christians for twenty centuries to some of history's most extraordinary feats of sacrifice and service to humanity. Christians should frequently proclaim the gospel's amazing core message, and even cautiously mention its positive out workings.

In addressing this fantastic vision, I have drawn on some very bright Christian writers, among them C. S. Lewis and E. L. Mascall. Mascall in particular articulates this vision comprehensively and beautifully.[2] I summarize some of his thoughts here.

Each Christian becomes a part of Christ's body, which process now in part, and eventually in total, will raise humanity and our world and "the heavens" into ecstatic, fully happy life with God forever. In addition, all of humanity is affected by this awesome "raising"; and they too will share in it, because Jesus, being man, is a gift, not just for those with "membership" but for any who will finally receive it.

Since at least the third century this Body, the Christian church, has been seriously distracted from such a vision by its pursuit of property, promotion, and social acceptance. This degradation has

---

2. See Mascall, *The Christian Universe*.

included building hierarchy and establishing traditions that encourage confusion and hypocrisy. Yet many Christians believe that the gathering of believers on Sunday to "eat and drink of Christ's body and blood" represents a literal ongoing connection with Christ among humans. All they do is tied to his atoning death in the first century. Thus they believe that nothing in existence here offers more hope of glory for humankind than this humble meal shared with them by God.

Writing on this meal, Mascall quotes John Betjeman's poem "Christmas."

> And is it true, and is it true,
> Seen in a stained-glass window's hue,
> A Baby in an ox's stall?
> The Maker of the Stars and Sea
> Become a Child on earth for me?
> And is it true? For if it is . . .
> No love that in a family dwells, no caroling in frosty air,
> Nor all the steeple-shaking bells, can with this single truth compare—
> That God was man in Palestine, and lives today in Bread and Wine.

I am a serious historical Christian but also committed to a broader perspective of that historic faith. I am also a grateful twelve-step practicer of the Adult Child type. For me there is no single setting in which these two life-enhancing walks coalesce more poignantly than at the Lord's Table, or Communion. There my historic faith urges upon me both intimate relating to the one whom I understand as a compassionate, suffering God-man, and also the total impact of all Twelve Steps. This means personal devotion, surrender, self-examination, and accountability for service and benevolence toward God and my fellow humans.

I believe I am made right with God by his sacrifice celebrated at that table. This is much like Step Three, in which I respond in faith by giving my life and will over to his care. My faith forms in me aspects of God-reality reflected only indirectly in the Steps. But the Steps, in turn, connect with me as an Adult Child through specific psychological insights that align my soul with God and others in helpful ways. I am a sinner "saved by grace," but the twelve-step program greatly aids me in the specific outworkings of that salvation. The most important of these is the frequent avoidance of making some desired objective a substitute for God—also known as idolatry.

SPIRITUAL RESOURCES FOR A PERILOUS FUTURE

The Christian church is in decline in Western culture, but on fire with expanding renewal in Asia and the Southern Hemisphere. Its growth there is more broadly expansive than at any other time in Christian history. Who knows what movements or positive cultural or political developments may result from this great spiritual energy? I urge the reader of this book and other spiritual literature to be alert to these developments, and to seriously consider joining such movements to participate in God's raising of his hopeful image in the world. We will need all the participation we can get as we prepare for a future filled with frightening challenges like irrational secularism and militant Islam, and perhaps fundamentalism of a Christian kind.

I intend to finish these observations about the gospel with brief remarks about humanity's eternal destiny, for this is the grand point of Jesus's reconnecting human beings and God. As the Apostle Paul said in the passage quoted earlier, there is literally no comparison between the present life and the next, either in duration or fullness. Granted, these assertions of eternal glory are startling, but here I will mention only one of Jesus's many statements about why this fabulous outcome seems to be taking so long. In the Gospel of Matthew Jesus says, "The kingdom of heaven is like leaven which a woman took and hid in . . . the meal, until it was all leavened" (13:34). This parable sums up his many teachings about our world's end. It describes the complex, lengthy process of mixing God's mind back into humanity's consciousness until it is all "leavened." Jesus taught that his kingdom would come by love's power, not by force, so lots of time is needed. Dorothy Sayers reflects on this beautifully in her poem "The Choice of the Cross."

> Hard it is, very hard,
> To travel up the slow and stony road
> To Calvary, to redeem mankind; far better
> To make but one resplendent miracle,
> Lean through the cloud, lift the right hand of power
> And with a sudden lightning smite the world perfect.
> Yet this was not God's way, Who had the power,
> But set it by, choosing the cross, the thorn,
> The sorrowful wounds. Something there is, perhaps,
> That power destroys in passing, something supreme,
> To whose great value in the eyes of God
> That cross, that thorn, and those five wounds bear witness.[3]

This poem and the paragraph before it summarize everything that the New Testament envisions both for the times immediately ahead of us and for their long-term scenario. But the New Testament also says much more to give hope to those who will live committedly through these times.

One solution to the great complexity of these mysteries is to simply and briefly declare what I think the New Testament visions of our era's outcome mean. I will then try to connect these stupendous coming events to our life decisions: to answer this question in light of such things, what is the best possible response?

Matthew 24:24,29-31 records the outline of the future that Jesus gave us. In it he essentially says that the global spread of his gospel will bring about "the end of the [evil] age." He continues by saying that "the powers of the heavens will be shaken." Then he declares that "the sign of the Son of Man" will appear and that he will send his angels to gather all his own into his kingdom reign. Paul and John especially expand on this general futuristic vision in texts such as Romans 8-11; Ephesians 1; 2 Thessalonians 2; and Revelation 16-20. All of these passages fit together with Jesus's threefold prophecy of the global spread of his gospel, the destruction of

---

3. Sayers, "The Choice of the Cross," *The Devil to Pay*.

Humanity beyond Sobriety, Time-Space, and Death

Satan's hidden evil influence in humanity's collective mind, and the ascendancy of Jesus's influence in us and in the cosmos.

From Jesus's language it is clear that the world is currently nearing the end of the first epoch he foretells—the global spread of his gospel. This means that we are rapidly approaching the second stage, climactic conflict with evil, which will issue in the third stage—the elevation of his kingdom. We will all need to prepare for the impending tumultuous time that will lead to Jesus's worldwide kingdom.

These visions look quite mysterious, but they mean that our human nature is the battlefield on which our world's future will be decided. There is a popular end-times view that says that God will soon come out of the sky and obliterate our problems for us by sheer overwhelming force. I obviously reject that view and contend instead that we are being called upon to work out our future with God's help as these prophecies hopefully describe it. For this reason I will explore a little further how we might practically cooperate with the great energy at work in this gospel vision.

All movements that lift and free the human soul from its suffering and hopelessness deserve our serious consideration. In the near future God's "people power" will increase dramatically; and, I believe, it will be offered widely. The spiritual energy described in these biblical pictures will expand powerfully in the near—chaotic—future. In practical terms, we face a future laced with unparalleled opportunity and also with great danger. The opportunity lies in our God-given creative gifts, and the danger lies in our tendency to see power as the greatest goal to be attained in the use of them. Dominance economically, militarily, or by terrorism is an irresistible idol. The biblical visions we've glimpsed urge us to put our hope in God's love as the primary purpose and guide for our technology and talent. The gist of the biblical vision for us, collectively and individually, is that our fear-driven perception of reality is unreal and cosmic in nature. At our core we fear being alone in this existence. We are powerless before this universal human insanity; it lies buried, too subtly and too far down, in our deep mind. Our choice is between "a Power greater" than this that lives in us or power as our god; between God and his care or the god of this power-driven world. The AA view and the gospel that is its mother are real and true—God has not withheld from us the best part of life, as the serpent in Genesis suggested. Our existence is covered in his greater power and care.

I am neither a futurist like the Tofflers[4] nor a prophet, but I can pray and read, habits I have practiced for seven decades. When I study the evolving cultural dynamics of my country and these biblical visions side by side, despair and hope contend for dominance in my mind. The news feeds despair; the visions, hope. The source of hope in these visions is the same as that which is found in the Twelve Steps: it is the fact that life under God's care is the most real of all existences for those who honestly want to be "clean and sober." God is with those who turn their lives over to his care, and always will be. Jesus said the same thing, that he was ascending to God and descending to us simultaneously (see the last four chapters in John's vision in his Apocalypse). The world was to go through tribulations, but no power in existence could prevent it from arriving at its final goal of life fully rejoined with his Father in eternity.

The poignant message of these New Testament visions is that God's power will be *with us* as our world struggles over what is most valuable and most real. In short, the visions declare that God has set in motion a spiritual energy capable of changing us into new, life-building men and women. Otherwise, our energies will be fatally absorbed by our deteriorating cities and families, our largely amoral media, our political statism, and our idolization of these and other aspects of our social life. These are vital areas of human existence where God's interventions are currently and always offering unique hope. It is in these on-the-ground arenas that human powerlessness—a powerlessness that we must admit—opens to us a blessed paradox: that our need for God is in itself empowering. But I believe these visions indicate that this long historical conflict will boil into global conflict in the next two

---

4. See Alvin Toffler, *Future Shock*; and Alvin and Heidi Toffler, *War and Anti-War*.

Humanity beyond Sobriety, Time-Space, and Death

centuries. It will be dangerous and difficult, and trusting God will be important. The church will suffer losses and experience dynamic renewals, but in the end, its essential spiritual power will remain undefeated (John 16:7–8).

It would be impractical to list all the social healing movements of the last century or those that will come from this power in the next two. The kinds of spiritual energy involved may be more than sociological. It well may be the kind of rational vision that formed America's constitutional government and successfully opposed Nazism and Communism. The story of Alcoholics Anonymous represents the marvelous possibilities of such widely available spiritual energy. The book *Serenity* by Robert Hemfelt and Richard Fowler tells this story with great care and insight. It hypothesizes a template for God's continuing vital involvement with humans in a world of trouble. Hemfelt and Fowler reflect more broadly on the story and its connection with Christ's gospel in the Oxford Movement: "All the movements of the church beginning with Peter and Paul and the other apostles had as their goal a spiritual awakening or renewal. This was true through the various monastic movements, the Protestant Reformation and the Oxford Movement of the early 1800s."[5] And to this list the Oxford Group, out of which the Twelve Steps developed, can be added.

Putting it all together, I believe we can foresee that this and the next few centuries will bring a world of trouble and opportunity. The trouble will come from humanity's blind subservience to cosmic forces whose appeal is to power as life's real solution. The opportunity will come from God's relentless, concrete offerings of love- and faith-based solutions.

All in all, the New Testament in its penetrating vision declares that this fast-approaching, unprecedented time of turbulence is also full of hope. The main cause of this hope is in the laws of God, which no rational being can successfully disregard for very long. The world was created to be actuated and fulfilled in God's love and rationality. Jesus taught two great governing principles in relation to this: The first is that Satan, "the thief," "comes only to steal

---

5. Hemfelt and Fowler, *Serenity*, 16.

and kill and destroy" (John 10:10). Read as an accurate description of the cosmic backdrop to the human dilemma, this insight says that evil and its captain never build, they only destroy. This is what the first three Steps are about; the fear-driven life tries to seize power from God's creative energy, and the First Step opposes this usurpation without exception.

This universal dynamic is seen in the dramatic New Testament end-times visions of everything coming to a head collectively and globally. The other prophecy Jesus gave along these lines is in his last words (John 16:6–11). He said that he would send the Holy Spirit at his ascension to "convince the world of sin and righteousness and judgment" (v. 8). This doesn't only apply to individuals who need spiritual renewal, though the Spirit's work is the mechanism that brings about new life. This is a great historic prediction that the world of our collective humanity will be changed by Christ's Spirit acting through his gospel. This prediction is what is described in all the end-times visions; it is happening now and will continue relentlessly in our world's future. Satan steals from this energy, but he is only able to wreak havoc with it. Take, for example, Communist China. The government brutally suppressed Christianity for decades. But a few decades later, the gospel began spreading there as it never had anywhere else in history. Principle: Satan's destructiveness produced only a hunger that God's care alone can satisfy.

We will face turbulence from the evil ahead, but it will come to a good end, the Christian visions predict. This is largely because the evil energy cannot permanently satisfy anything in our humanity. That fulfillment will come only to the people who believe in a Power greater than themselves and decide to turn their lives and their wills over to the care of God.

All that is wrong in our land springs from opposition to this First Step. The force of this Step's dynamic will bear down on that opposition, because humans were created to live in harmony with their Creator. The strain of disharmonious living leads to the necessity of the first three Steps. Therefore, some of us are living by these gospel-driven Steps, and have hope for our children and

Humanity beyond Sobriety, Time-Space, and Death

others', and for our land, that this tension will have the effect of "convincing the world of sin and righteousness and judgment."

So we go forward in our recovering families convinced that we and our world are under God's care. We will go on seeking—and urge all who are concerned to go on seeking—God's kingdom and his righteousness first, and all else after that. Find those parts of his renewal energy that emerge in your area of life, and support and join renewal where you live. There will be much of it, and God's energy will be powerful and prolific if we are willing to seek and knock and enter.

We are going to pass through the storm ahead one way or another; we might as well do it with his promise and his care. The church and other good institutions may be brought low, and darkness may spread frighteningly. Western societies will have to hit their "bottom" just as individuals do. Among several cryptic sayings of Jesus about this historic climax is one in the Revelation of John: "Behold I am coming like a thief. Blessed is the one who stays awake . . . lest . . . men see his shame" (16:15). The decades ahead will not be "business as usual." A terrific moral crisis is now upon the Western world, yes, on all peoples of the globe. It is time for ordinary people to seriously commit their lives to some way of seeking and serving God's purposes. Serving God will not disappoint. Serving self always will. But this principle of judgment leads to renewal—always. "Our God is marching on"—that old "Battle Hymn of the Republic" will turn out to be even truer now than when it was written. A great, fabulous future lies ahead of this storm, say the biblical and twelve-step visionaries, "for God so loved the world" (John 3:16), and God's care is the most trustworthy promise in existence for any person and any kind of world. As this moral crisis develops, God will intervene with saving actions and quickenings to prepare more of us individually (and anonymously) to be able to recognize the King and his kingdom of life as its day begins to dawn. As we pass from this tiny life into that larger one, we will be able to see his love and will be transfigured by it. For the answer to this question will be the key to every human's eternal relating to God: will their soul be open to the love of God in such a way that they value that dynamic above all else in existence? This assessment will be part of every soul's self-awareness to a greater or lesser degree. God, in his judgment, will be totally aware of this core state of the heart in each human being. He will know simply whether we have decided to be God ourselves or to acknowledge God as God. He will know if we can recognize which is which. Your eternity will not be decided by your record on earth; it will be decided finally by your real response to God. Every occurrence of a newly "born" human soul, clean and sober, is a living parable in our world of response to that other world.

Bibliography

Banks, Robert. *Paul's Idea of Community: The Early House Churches in Their Historical Setting.* Grand Rapids: Eerdmans, 1980.

Hemfelt, Robert, and Richard Fowler. *Serenity: A Companion for Twelve Step Recovery.* Nashville: Thomas Nelson, 1990.

Jenkins, Philip. *The Next Christendom: The Coming of Global Christianity.* New York: Oxford University Press, 2002.

Lewis, C. S. *The Allegory of Love: A Study in Medieval Tradition.* London: Oxford University Press, 1977.

———. *Made for Heaven: How the Christian Life Works.* San Francisco: HarperOne, 2005.

Manning, Brennan. *Abba's Child: The Cry of the Heart for Intimate Belonging.* Colorado Springs: NavPress, 1994.

Mascall, E. L. *The Christian Universe.* New York: Morehouse-Barlow, 1966.

Milt, Harry. *The Revised Basic Handbook on Alcoholism.* Maplewood, New Jersey: Scientific Aids, 1977.

Nee, Watchman. *The Normal Christian Life.* Wheaton, Illinois: Tyndale, 1977.

Peterson, Eugene. *The Message: The Bible in Contemporary Language.* Colorado Springs: NavPress, 2005.

Polkinghorne, Dr. John. *The God of Hope and the End of the World.* New Haven, Connecticut: Yale University Press, 2003.

Rohr, Richard. *Breathing Under Water.* Cincinnati: St. Anthony Messenger, 2011.

Sayers, Dorothy L. "The Choice of the Cross." *The Devil to Pay.* (Publishing information not accessible.)

Toffler, Alvin. *Future Shock.* New York: Random House, 1970.

———, and Heidi Toffler. *War and Anti-War: Survival at the Dawn of the 21st Century.* Boston: Little, Brown, and Co., 1993.

Twelve Steps and Twelve Traditions. New York: A.A. World Services, 1953.

W., Bill. *Alcoholic Anonymous.* New York: A.A. World Services, 1939.

Bibliography

Woititz, Janet G. *Adult Children of Alcoholics*. Pompano Beach, Florida: Health Communications, 1983.

www.ingramcontent.com/pod-product-compliance
Lightning Source LLC
Chambersburg PA
CBHW051701090426
42736CB00013B/2481